AFRICAN AMERICAN INVENTORS & SCIENTISTS

AFRICAN AMERICAN INVENTORS & SCIENTISTS

T.M. Moody

African American Inventors and Scientists
African American History for Kids, #1

Copyright © 2022 T.M. Moody

All rights reserved. No part of this book may be reproduced or transmitted in any form or by any means without written permission of the publisher. For questions, contact us at info@thekulturekidz.com or visit our website at thekulturekidz.com for printables already designated for noncommercial use.

Paperback ISBN: 979-8417964824

Kulture Kidz Books
Tymm Publishing LLC
www.tymmpublishing.com

Editor: editorsylvia
Illustrations of Inventor Headshots: T.M. Moody
Cover and Interior Designer: TywebbinCreations.com

TABLE OF CONTENTS

Introduction	9
Benjamin Banneker	17
Dr. Patricia Bath	21
George Washington Carver	25
Marian Rogers Croak	31
Mark Dean	35
Dr. Charles Richard Drew	39
Granville T. Woods	43
Miriam Benjamin	51
Marie Van Brittan Brown	55
Sarah Boone	59
Sarah E. Goode	63
Lewis Howard Latimer	67
Elijah McCoy	71
Garrett Morgan	75
Madam C.J. Walker	79
Timeline	83
Glossary	87
Activity Book	93
About the Author	97
Kulture Kidz Books	99

INTRODUCTION

Are you interested in science?

Do you want to invent something new some day?

In this book, you will read about African American scientists, engineers, and extraordinary people who created items that shaped the world. You will learn about their life and how they came up with their inventions. As you read about each person, pay attention to words in bold. Those are vocabulary words. The book is split into two parts:

CAREERS IN STEM

This section focuses specifically on individuals who obtained degrees from higher education institutions. The goal is to show you their career path and achievements.

EXTRAORDINARY PEOPLE

Sometimes circumstances bring great ideas during everyday life. Meet people who saw a need or wanted to change their situation. Their inventions not only changed their world, but continue to help others today.

At the end of this book is a timeline, a glossary, and a bibliography for further research.

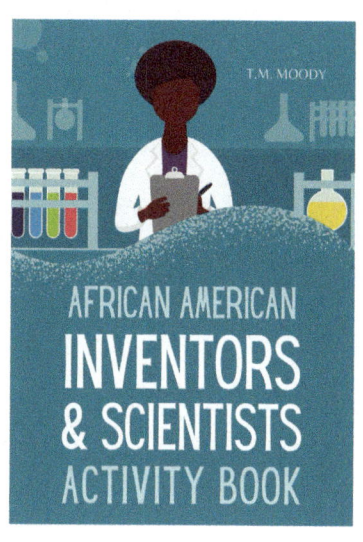

NOTE: *This book has a companion activity book.*

Find out how you can get a copy at TheKultureKidz.com/book

PART 1

CAREERS IN STEM

PART 1: CAREERS IN STEM

A career in the **STEM** field would involve having some knowledge of **s**cience, **t**echnology, **e**ngineering, and **m**ath. People with careers in STEM are problem-solvers and creative.

In the next few chapters, you will meet African American men and women who were and are scientists, doctors, engineers, and computer scientists. They stand out in history because they were among the first to research, explore and create some incredible inventions.

Many, if not most of them, didn't have an easy journey along the way. Sometimes people judge us by the color of our skin instead of giving us a chance to show what we really can do. You will read about people who pushed forward to create some of the things we see or use every day despite obstacles.

BENJAMIN BANNEKER

1731-1806

Have you ever looked up at the sky at night? What did you see and how did it make you feel? As a young boy growing up on a farm, we can imagine Benjamin Banneker's being curious about the sun, moon and all the stars in the sky.

That curiosity sparked a lifelong passion for astronomy.

Banneker is often known as the "First African American Scientist." Born in Maryland on November 9, 1731, Banneker's parents were formerly enslaved people making him a free African American. Banneker was able to go to a Quaker school near his home for a few years. **Quakers** are a group of people who believe all people are unique and equal. Since they believe no one should be harmed or threatened, many Quakers were **abolitionists**, people who worked to end slavery.

When he grew older and could no longer attend school, Banneker had to learn new things on his own. That wasn't a problem for Banneker. One of his first achievements was building a wooden clock that worked for over 50 years. During Banneker's time, most clocks were built overseas in Europe. Some people thought his clock was the first working one in the United States.

Banneker grew up on his family's 100-acre tobacco farm in Maryland. He continued to live on the farm as an adult so farming was pretty essential for him. He studied **astronomy** which is the study of everything in the universe like planets, stars, comets, and galaxies. His studies helped him publish an almanac every year.

An **almanac** is a book that includes a calendar and information about the sun, moon phases, ocean tides, and weather forecasts. This was a very helpful resource for farmers. Farmers have been and still use almanacs today to determine how the weather could affect their crops. For example, too much rain or not enough rain can damage crops.

Benjamin Banneker's Almanac was a top seller from Pennsylvania to Virginia and as far as Kentucky from 1792 to 1797. In 1791, Banneker sent a copy of his very first almanac to Thomas Jefferson. Jefferson was serving as Secretary of State for President George Washington. He would later become the third President of the United States.

Banneker sent a special letter along with the almanac to Jefferson. In his letter, Banneker wrote about how it wasn't fair to enslave people. Even though Jefferson was a slaveholder, he wrote back explaining that he'd begun to have a change of heart. Impressed with him, Jefferson recommended Banneker help survey or measure the land which is known as Washington, D.C. today.

After he died, Banneker's house caught on fire. The fire destroyed his famous wooden clock as well as many of Banneker's things. It's good that we're still able to know about all his achievements today.

Have you learned about the solar system in school yet?

Describe some of the things found in the solar system.

DR. PATRICIA BATH

1942-2019

Have you been to an eye doctor? If so, how did you do when you read the eye chart on the wall? Maybe you or someone you know has to wear glasses.

Dr. Patricia Bath was a female doctor who dedicated her life to making sure all people were able to receive eye care.

Dr. Bath was an **ophthalmologist**, a doctor who specializes in eye and vision care. As a young girl, she dreamed about becoming a doctor. She was an excellent student in school. In fact, by the time she was sixteen years old, Bath pursued her dream of becoming a doctor by attending Howard University College of Medicine in Washington, D.C. After graduating from medical school, Bath became an intern at Harlem Hospital in New York.

Interns, also known as first-year residents, are doctors. During their first year of practicing medicine, they have to be supervised while they are with patients. After the first year, the doctor begins a residency, which can last for 2-7 years. During the residency, the doctor is learning to become better and better at their specialty.

Dr. Bath's specialty during her residency was eye and vision care. She became the first African American resident in ophthalmology at New York University. During her residency, she noticed many of her patients were blind or visually impaired. Many of these patients were African Americans who had not been to see an eye doctor usually because they couldn't afford to go.

So passionate about eye care, Dr. Bath and three other colleagues founded the American Institute for the Prevention of Blindness (AIPB). The organization's goal was to make sure anyone, no matter their race or economic status had access to eye care.

She was also known as a laser scientist. A **laser** is an instrument that produces a powerful beam of light. With a lot of research, Dr. Bath invented the Laserphaco Probe, a tool that corrects cataracts during eye surgery. **Cataracts** are an eye condition that can lead to blindness, and Dr. Bath's tool provided a safe way to remove them.

When she patented the Laserphaco Probe in 1988, Dr. Bath became the first African American female doctor to secure a medical patent.

Did you know there are only two African American women who have been inducted into the National Inventors Hall of Fame? Dr. Bath was one of them. In this book, you will meet the other woman. Keep reading!

If you were a doctor, what would be your specialty?

GEORGE WASHINGTON CARVER

1860-1943

Have you've ever helped plant a garden? There is something special about planting a seed in soil and giving it proper care so it can grow healthy.

George Washington Carver loved learning about plants as a young boy. His passion for plant life and his desire to help people remained with him for the rest of his life.

In 1860, George was born into slavery on a farm near Diamond, Missouri. By the time George was five years old, slavery had been abolished with the 13th Amendment. Despite the amendment, it still took many years for all enslaved people to be fully free. George would suffer a big loss when slave raiders kidnapped his mother.

Moses Carver, a white farm owner, raised George and his younger brother, James. George would take "Carver" as his last name, something that many enslaved people did.

Both George and his brother learned how to read and write. His brother learned how to work on the farm, but George could not help out because he was always getting sick. Despite not being able to do much work, George was curious about plants.

His passion for growing healthy plants and crops stayed with him as he got older. He was encouraged to apply to Iowa State Agricultural School (now called Iowa State University). Once accepted at Iowa State, George studied botany.

In 1894, George became the first African American to receive a Bachelor of Science degree from Iowa

State. He didn't stop there. In 1896, George also earned a Master of Agriculture degree, making

CROP ROTATION METHOD

Year 1 - Cotton Plant Growing Process.
Graphic Credit: Andrii Bezvershenko, 123rf.com

Year 2 - Peanut Plant Growing Process.
Graphic Credit: Havryliuk-Kharzhevska. Shutterstock.com

another first in history.

George had become well known for his work with plants. The founder of Tuskegee Institute (University), Booker T. Washington, was looking to create a school of agriculture for African American students. He asked George to come work as the Agriculture Director at

Tuskegee. In 1896, George accepted the offer and worked at the school for the remainder of his life.

He invented many ways to help poor African American farmers harvest healthy crops using chemistry. **Crops** can be plants like vegetables, fruit, or grain or fiber like cotton. Cotton took a lot of the nutrients from the soil.

George created the **crop rotation method** for cotton farmers who had worn out their soil. Planting peanuts every other year made the soil better, adding more nutrients for the next round of crops.

Why peanuts? Peanuts are **legumes**, which are plants that produce a pod with seeds inside. Peanuts don't require a lot of water and grow underground. They produce **nitrogen**, a colorless and odorless gas that provides much-needed nutrients to the soil. While George is well-known for using peanuts, he also encouraged the use of other legumes as well like peas and black-eyed peas.

Did you know George created 325 different uses for the peanut? Now, most people think Carver invented peanut butter, but that's the one product that he didn't invent, even though he was known as "The Peanut Man." Carver not only worked with peanuts but also made several products from sweet potatoes too.

What kind of plants would you add if you could start a garden?

MARIAN ROGERS CROAK

1955 -

The World Wide Web is really a collection of pages. Billions of pages, in fact. When you want to search for a particular page, it's helpful to use a search engine. You may have used Google, a very popular search engine.

Google LLC is a large technology company that produces many types of internet products. During the time this book was written, Marian Rogers Croak worked as the Vice President of Engineering at Google.

Marian has come a long way from being a young girl who loved science. Marian was born in Pennsylvania on May 14, 1955, but grew up in New York City.

She attended Princeton University for her undergraduate studies. In 1982, she earned her doctorate from the University of Southern California. A **doctorate** is the highest degree a student can earn from a college or university. Marian focused on two areas, statistical analysis and social psychology. Statistical analysis is the science of collecting and exploring large amounts of data to find out if there are any patterns or trends. Social psychology is the science of studying how a person or a group of people's behavior may be affected by others.

You're probably thinking, how did Marian use her studies in her career. Not too long after she graduated in 1982, Marian began working at AT&T in the Human Factors Division department. Her job was to figure out how technology could help people.

It was during this time that Marian invented **Voice over Internet Protocol** or VoIP. **VoIP** is a type of technology that allows a person to talk on a phone using the internet. Later, Marian created a way for people to donate money to charities by using text messaging on the phone. In 2005 when Hurricane Katrina hit New Orleans, her invention helped people all over donate money easily to help the victims.

Marian has over 200 patents and loves encouraging young girls to pursue STEM careers.

By the way, remember in an earlier chapter, Dr. Patricia Bath was one of two African American women inducted into the National Inventors Hall of Fame. Well, Marian Rogers Croak is the other woman.

Can you think of an invention that would help people?

MARK DEAN

1957-

Computers are everywhere these days! They're even small enough to fit in your hand. Smartphones are really just small computers. There was a time when computers were as big as *a room, and not many people knew about them or how to use them.*

International Business Machines (IBM) Corporation was one of the first companies to start making personal computers in the early 1980s. Mark E. Dean is a computer scientist and engineer at IBM.

As a little boy, Mark loved building things. He was a straight A student and an athlete while in school. When it was time for him to go to college, he decided to study engineering at the University of Tennessee. Soon after he graduated, he started working for IBM.

Mark worked with another engineer, Dennis Moeller, during his early years at IBM to invent the Industry Standard Architecture (ISA). An ISA allows users to plug in devices to a computer like a printer or a disk drive.

Later, Mark's research helped him invent the color PC monitor. He also created the first gigahertz chip, which helps a computer process information really, really fast.

Mark has a total of nine patents. Like Dr. Patricia Bath and Marian Rogers Croak, Mark was inducted into the National Inventors Hall of Fame too.

He has another honor that's pretty special. In 1996, Mark was recognized as an IBM Fellow. Becoming an

IBM Fellow is the highest honor a scientist, engineer, or programmer at IBM can achieve. Mark E. Dean was the first African American to receive this honor.

What's something you would like to invent to make computers even better to use?

DR. CHARLES RICHARD DREW

1904-1950

Have you ever had your blood taken by a nurse? It can hurt at first to fill that needle in your arm.

A lot can be learned about what's going on in your body when your blood is tested.

Blood is really important for our bodies. The reddish liquid can bring oxygen and nutrients to all parts of our body. Imagine what could happen if you are hurt and lose a lot of blood.

Dr. Charles Richard Drew was known as the "Father of the Blood Bank." He was born in Washington, DC, where he lived with his four younger siblings. Drew's interest in becoming a doctor began after his younger sister died from a disease called tuberculosis. An excellent student and athlete, Drew was accepted and attended Amherst College in Massachusetts.

His dream of becoming a doctor began when Drew was accepted into the McGill University Faculty of Medicine in Montreal, Quebec. Quebec is a province in Canada, with Montreal being one of its largest cities. Dr. Drew graduated second in his class in 1933. During his time as a medical intern, he became interested in **transfusion** or how blood is transferred.

After completing his internship, he returned back home to Washington, D.C., where he began his career at Howard University. His work at Howard University led him to learn how to **preserve** or safely store blood

plasma, the largest part of blood, for long periods of time.

Dr. Drew became the first director of the American Red Cross blood bank. He didn't stay in this position too long, though. Dr. Drew resigned because he didn't like that the Red Cross participated in segregation. **Segregation** is setting one group of people apart from another group. Most of the time, one group was treated unfairly. Even though Dr. Drew parted ways, his work saved thousands of lives during World War II, and the Red Cross continues to use his system today.

Dr. Drew was killed in a car crash on his way to a medical conference in Tuskegee, Alabama. He'd been up most of the night working and fell asleep while driving. In 1966, the Charles R. Drew University of Medicine and Science was established in Los Angeles, California.

Do you know the different types of blood?

GRANVILLE T. WOODS

1856- 1910

An engineer can design or build some pretty complex things like machines, systems, or structures. A person who becomes an engineer often has to learn *various sciences like physics, chemistry, and/or biology to understand how things work.*

In 1856, Granville T. Woods was born to free African American parents in Columbus, Ohio. After the Civil War, Granville became the first African American mechanical and electrical engineer.

He started his own company to **manufacture** or make a large number of electrical devices. His most famous invention was the multiplex telegraph. A **telegraph** lets people send messages using code and electronics. Granville's device made it possible for people to talk over telegraph wires.

You may have heard of the famous American inventor Thomas Edison. He was probably the most famous electrical engineer during his time. Some of his inventions include the incandescent light bulb, the phonograph, and the motion picture camera. Edison also worked on improvements to early versions of the telegraph and telephone.

Edison sued Granville for his telegraph invention, claiming that he was the one who'd invented the telegraph first. After a hard battle in the courts, Granville won his patent.

Today, he is often known as the "Black Edison." Granville's legacy is sound, and during his lifetime, he registered almost 60 patents.

Granville liked building electronics. What's something you want to learn how to build?

PART 2

EXTRAORDINARY PEOPLE

PART 2: EXTRAORDINARY PEOPLE

Determination: *A quality that makes you continue trying to do or achieve something that is difficult. (Merriam-Webster Dictionary)*

In the first part of this book, you met individuals who have careers in science, engineering, medicine, or computer science. While being good at science or technology is awesome, determination can go a long way in making your idea a reality.

In the next few chapters, you will meet extraordinary people who came up with ideas, sometimes out of frustration or wanting to see something different happen in their lives. We can learn a lot from their determination to make a difference.

"I had to make my own living and my own opportunity. But I made it! Don't sit down and wait for the opportunities to come. Get up and make them."

- Madam C. J. Walker

MIRIAM BENJAMIN

1861-1947

How do you feel about crowds? Sometimes it's not easy to be seen or heard when you are around a group of people. It can get pretty noisy when everyone is trying to talk at the same time.

Miriam Elizabeth Benjamin came up with a simple idea that continues to be used today. Born in Charleston, South Carolina, Miriam's family later moved to Boston, Massachusetts. When Miriam grew up, she became a teacher. She must have really enjoyed learning because she earned both a medical and a law degree from Howard University.

While Miriam lived and worked in Washington, DC, she came up with her a very helpful invention. In 1888, Miriam invented a special type of chair called a Gong and Signal Chair for Hotels. To see how the chair worked, look at the image below.

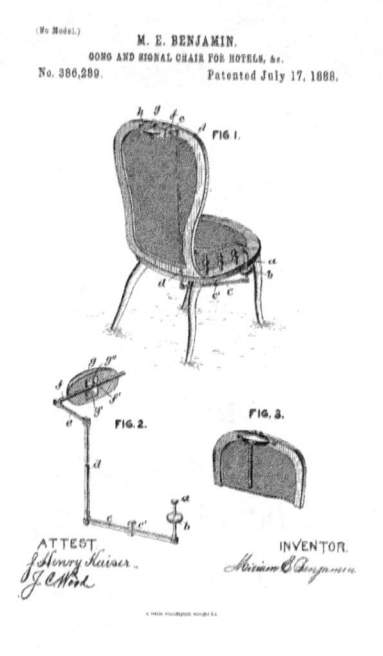

A small button could be found on the side of the chair (see Fig. 1). When the person touched the button, it rang a bell (see Fig. 2) and also displayed a red ball in the back of the chair (see Fig. 3). This helped hotel waiters know which guests needed help.

Miriam thought her invention would work great in other places like hospitals, theaters, and even for legislators. **Legislators** are members of a body that create laws. Later, a similar type of system was set up for the U.S. House of Representatives, which is the lower branch of Congress.

If you ever go on a airplane, Miriam's invention has been adapted as a flight attendant call button. Passengers can press this button to ask a flight attendant for help. It's located above the passenger, usually next to the reading light and air nozzles. It is recommended to use the call button for emergencies only so be nice to your flight attendant.

Miriam became the second African American woman to be awarded a patent. A **patent** gives the inventor the right to be the only maker of a product for a certain number of years.

What amazing invention can you make that uses a button? How can it help people?

MARIE VAN BRITTAN BROWN

1922-1999

Have you ever been afraid? What were you afraid of, and what did you do to overcome your fear? Sometimes things happen in the world, which makes it a scary place to be, but your parents, teachers, and many people are there to help you remain safe.

Marie Van Brittan Brown lived in Queens, New York, where at the time, the crime rate was pretty high. She worked as a nurse and lived with her husband, Albert Brown, who was an electrician. Sometimes Marie was in the house by herself, and she didn't like not knowing what was going on outside her house. She decided that she didn't want to be afraid all the time about her safety.

Marie and Albert worked together to invent the first home security system. The couple was awarded the patent in 1966.

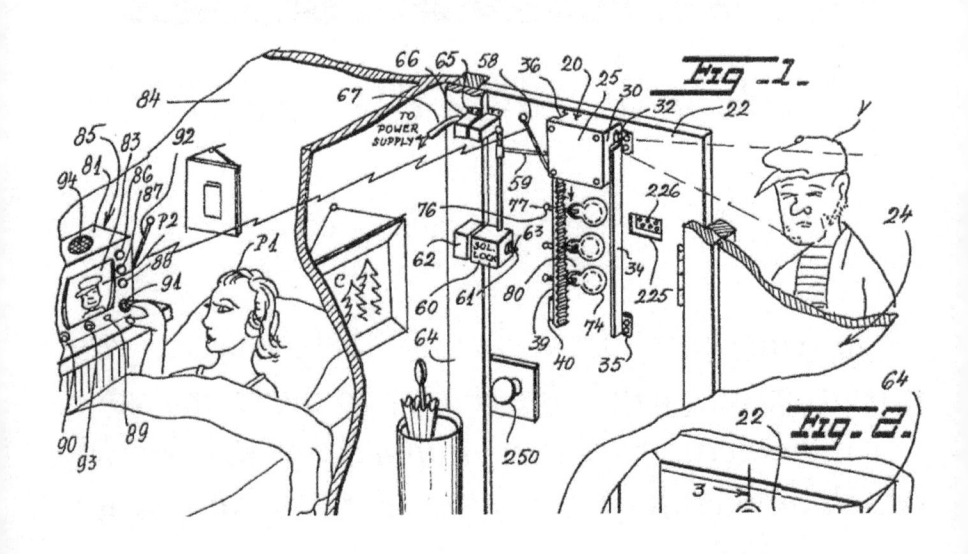

The home security system allowed Marie to see anyone at the front door using peepholes and camera monitors. There was a two-way microphone that allowed her to talk to people as well. If Marie sensed any trouble, there was an alarm button that could be pressed to contact the police. Most home security systems today work pretty similarly to her version.

Marie shows us that when something makes us afraid, we can do something about it. In her case, she invented something that other people can use to make them feel safe too.

What if you can build an invention to help people? What would it be, and how would it help?

SARAH BOONE

1832-1904

Do you have an ironing board at your house? Irons can get pretty hot, so you have to be careful. Adults may not want you to use it until you are older. Did you know, even if a product exists, if you can make it work better, that's an invention too. Sarah Boone, a dressmaker, decided to make a change to the ironing board she used every day.

Sarah Boone was born in North Carolina. She lived during the 19th century, which was from January 1, 1801 – December 31, 1900. A century is one hundred (100) years. Do you know the name of the century you are living in right now?

This book was published in 2022. The start of this century began January 1, 2001, and will last until December 31, 2100. That makes this the 21st century.

Back to Sarah's time! She grew up to be a dressmaker. Now Sarah didn't just make dresses, but she made all kinds of clothes for women like skirts, shirts, coats and more. A popular style during Sarah's time was a suit that had a fitted jacket along with a long, slim skirt. After clothes were sewn, they often had wrinkles in them and had to be smoothed out on an ironing board so they would fit properly.

Ironing boards had been around for a while, but Sarah decided to make a change to the ironing board she used all the time. She figured out a way to iron sleeves as well as the bodies of women's garments (another name for clothes) without leaving ugly creases. Sarah had help building her ironing board from her husband, James Boone, who was a carpenter.

Her ironing board looks a little different from the ones you see today. Check out her ironing board below.

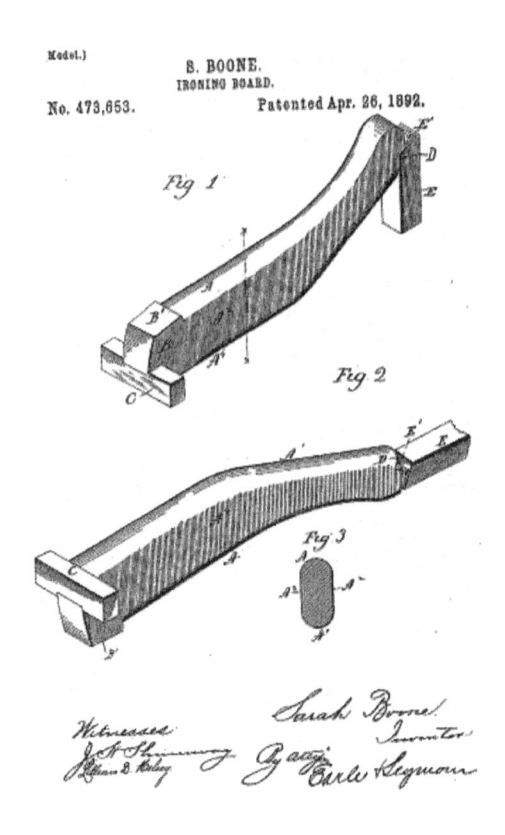

It was made out of wood, and you could fit a sleeve inside the narrow curve. The sleeve could easily be flipped over without making creases.

In 1892, her invention was approved, making her one of the first African American women to be awarded a patent.

Is there something around you that you can improve or make better like Sarah?

SARAH E. GOODE

1850-1905

You may have a special room in your house for guests. In some guest bedrooms there are couches that can open up into beds. Pretty convenient!

There is not much information about Sarah E. Goode, not even a photo. What we do know is Sarah became one of the first African American women to receive a **patent** after she invented the Folding Cabinet Bed.

Being able to **draft** or draw your idea is an important skill so you can present your ideas. Sarah had some help from her husband, who was a carpenter. Check out the drawing below.

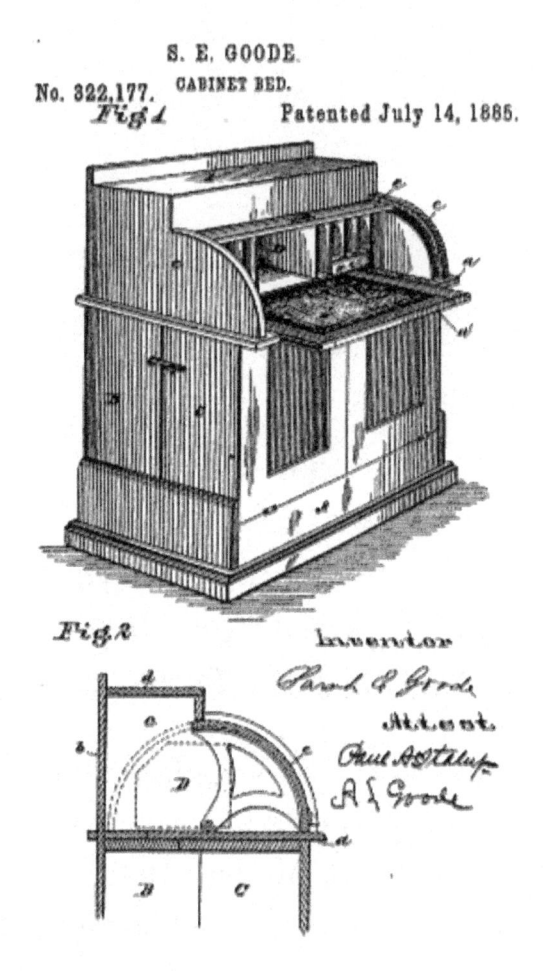

S. E. GOODE.
CABINET BED.
No. 322,177.
Fig 1.
Patented July 14, 1885.

Sarah's folding cabinet bed worked like a sofa or a hideaway bed that is used today. This bed was perfect for small rooms and pretty unique too because when it was folded up, it became a desk with cool places to put stuff. A bed that turns into a desk. Wow!

What would you turn your bed into? Do you have any ideas for other furniture in your house?

LEWIS HOWARD LATIMER

1848-1928

Do you enjoy going to school? What are some of your favorite subjects? Having an education can help you fulfill your dreams of becoming who you want to be when you grow up.

Lewis Howard Latimer wasn't able to get an education, but the lack of schooling didn't stop him from learning. While he was in the Navy, he taught himself to become a **draftsman**, a person who can make mechanical drafts or drawings that show how a machine works. Lewis' skills led him to work with two famous inventors.

Latimer worked as an assistant to Alexander Graham Bell and played an important role in the creation of the telephone. He used his skills to create the drawings for the patent that Bell submitted in 1876. Yeah, the drawing doesn't look like phones today.

Later, Latimer also worked with Thomas Edison. He invented something called a carbon filament. This small piece helped make incandescent light bulbs work. **Incandescent** bulbs glow or give light from being heated. It was easier to produce the carbon filament, so a lot more people could use light bulbs.

An incandescent light bulb is made of glass on the outside. All of the air inside the glass bulb has been sucked out. Inside the bulb is a thin wire called a filament. Latimer made this filament out of carbon, but today it's made out of another metal called tungsten. Once the light bulb is connected to electricity, the electricity travels up the base to the support wires and then to the filament. Once the filament gets very hot, then the light bulb starts to give light.

While Latimer helped out two great inventors, he also had his own inventions, which included an "improved railroad car bathroom and an early air conditioning unit."

Is there a famous person that you would like to work with someday?

ELIJAH MCCOY

1844-1929

Have you ever rode on a train? In the 1800s, trains became a major form of transportation. They offered a quick way to travel from one place to the other.

Elijah McCoy was born May 2, 1844, in Colchester, Ontario. His parents, George and Mildred, were formerly enslaved people who escaped from Kentucky with help from the Underground Railroad.

The **Underground Railroad** was a method that helped enslaved people escape from the South to the North during the mid-1800s. The passengers did not travel on a real train, nor did they go underground. They traveled by whatever means they could, moving during the nighttime and hiding during the daytime in safe houses. Elijah would grow up to make a great invention for real railroads.

His first invention, an automatic lubricating cup, was used in steam cylinders of trains and other machinery. The lubricating cup spread oil evenly over a train's engine while it moved. This allowed a train to run for long periods of time without stopping.

Elijah was awarded over 57 **patents** during his lifetime and became known as one of the great African American inventors of the 19th century.

Are you interested in vehicles like automobiles, trains, boats, or airplanes? Maybe you would like to see how they are designed and built.

GARRETT MORGAN

1877-1963

Do you ride a bus to school? Maybe one of your parents will drop you off in a car. Probably at some point on your route, you have to stop at a traffic light. Did you know an African American man invented the traffic light?

Garrett Augustus Morgan was born in Paris, Kentucky. He was the seventh of eleven children. Garrett went to Cincinnati, Ohio, to look for work during his teenage years. He didn't have a lot of education but was determined to learn. After working at several **factories** where products are made, Garrett started to get his own ideas. He received his first patent for improving how a sewing machine worked. Soon he opened his own business.

Garrett's main business was to make repairs on sewing machines, but he soon discovered a new idea. Sometimes needles cause problems, especially when working with a fabric like wool. Garrett worked with some chemicals to make the needle go through the wool fabric easier. He noticed the chemicals had an interesting effect on the wool cloth. It not only made the needle work better, but it made the wool straight.

That gave Garrett an idea. What if the chemical could be used on human hair, specifically African American hair, to make it straight. He tried it out on himself, and soon, he had a new hair cream that became very popular. He started a new business, G.A.

Morgan Hair Refining Company. Now Garrett didn't stop with this idea. There were more inventions to come.

Garrett was really good at thinking about and creating inventions that could help people. In 1914, Morgan received a patent for an invention called a safety hood. This hood could be worn over the head and helped the person breathe better when there was smoke or gasses in the air. Garrett really wanted fire departments to use the breathing device when they had to fight fires. He had some trouble getting people to take him seriously due to the color of his skin.

There was a horrible natural gas explosion in 1916. Workers had been drilling a new tunnel under Lake Erie and had become trapped. Morgan heard about the explosion and used his safety hood to help save lives that day. His breathing device was later adapted for the gas masks used during World War I.

You see one of his most famous inventions everyday when you are in a car. It was common to see a horse and carriage on the road during Garrett's time. Cars were still new, and not a lot of people had them yet. In 1923, Garrett saw a really bad accident in the city. The accident inspired him to create a three-way traffic light so people would know when to stop and let the other vehicle drive through first.

Versions of Garrett's gas mask and traffic light are being used today.

What is something you can invent to help people?

MADAM C.J. WALKER

1867-1919

Today, African American girls can wear their hair in an assortment of hairstyles. They can wear braids, afro puffs, afros, twists, ponytails, etc. Hairstyles are limitless! Madam C. J. Walker would influence how African American women styled their hair.

Born Sarah Breedlove in 1867, she was the daughter of Louisiana sharecroppers. **Sharecropping** was a hard life where farmers had to give the landowner a portion of their crop. Sarah began working as a laundress. With this job, she washed and ironed clothing as well as bed linens.

While Sarah worked as a laundress, she started having trouble with her hair falling out. By mixing several different oils together in a washtub, she created a hairdressing **formula** or a recipe. The formula gave African American women a new way to wear their hair by straightening their tight curls. "Madam Walker's Wonderful Hair Grower made a major change in the hair industry for African American women.

In 1905, she invented and patented a straightening comb, which, when heated and used with her hairdressing formula, changed tightly curled hair into shiny straight hair.

By 1919, the Madam C.J. Walker Manufacturing Company stretched an entire city block and provided employment for over 3,000 people. This **entrepreneur** went from being a laundress to

America's first self-made African American millionaire businesswoman.

If you could start your own business, what would you do?

TIMELINE

The 1700s

1731 - Benjamin Banneker was born in Maryland on November 9, 1731

1791 - Benjamin Banneker sent a copy of his very first almanac to Thomas Jefferson

The 1800s

1872 - Elijah McCoy received his first patent for an automatic lubricating device.

1876 - Lewis Latimer used his drafting skills to create the patent drawings for Alexander Graham Bell's telephone.

1887 - Granville T. Woods invented the multiplex telegraph.

1888 - Miriam Benjamin invented the Gong and Signal Chair for Hotels.

1892- Sarah Boone became one of the first African American women to be awarded a patent.

1896 - George Washington Carver became the Agriculture Director at Tuskegee Institute (University).

The 1900s

1906 - Madam C. J. Walker's Wonderful Hair Grower became available for purchase

1941 - Dr. Charles R. Drew became the first director of the American Red Cross blood bank.

1966 - The Charles R. Drew University of Medicine and Science was established in Los Angeles, California.

1966 - Marie Van Brittan Brown and her husband, Albert, were awarded a patent for their home security system.

1988 - Dr. Patricia Bath became the first African American female doctor to secure a medical patent for her Laserphaco Probe.

1996 - Mark E. Dean was recognized as an IBM Fellow. He was the first African American to receive this honor.

The 2000s

2005 - When Hurricane Katrina hit New Orleans, Marian Rogers Croak's invention helped people all over donate money using text messaging.

GLOSSARY

Several vocabulary words were introduced throughout the book. Below you can find a review of definitions and also how to say the words out loud. Some of these are great words to know if you are ever in a spelling bee!

Abolitionists (a-buh-li-shuh-nuhsts) - people who worked to end slavery

Almanac (aal-muh-nak) - A book that includes a calendar and information about the sun, moon phases, ocean tides, and weather forecasts.

Astronomy (uh-straa-nuh-mee) - The study of everything in the universe like planets, stars, comets, and galaxies.

Cataracts (ka-tr-akts) - An eye condition that can lead to blindness.

Crops - Plants like vegetables, fruit, or grain or fiber like cotton.

Doctorate (daak-tr-uht) - The highest degree a student can earn from a college or university.

Draftsman (drafts-muhn) - A person who can make mechanical drafts or drawings that show how a machine works.

Entrepreneur (aan-truh-pruh-noor) - A person who creates and runs their own business.

Factories (fak-tr-eez) - A place where products are made.

Formula (for-myuh-luh) - A list of ingredients or steps for making a product.

Incandescent (in-kuhn-deh-snt) - To glow or give light from being heated. Example: Light bulb

Legislators (leh-juh-slay-trz) - Members of a body that create laws.

Legumes (leh-gyoomz) - Plants that produce a pod with seeds inside. Peanuts are a legume.

Manufacture (ma-nyoo-fak-chr) - To make a large number of products.

Nitrogen (nai-truh-jn) - A colorless and odorless gas that provides much-needed nutrients to the soil.

Ophthalmologist (aaf-thuh-maa-luh-juhst) - A doctor who specializes in eye and vision care

Quakers (kway-krz) - Believe all people are unique and equal, and many were abolitionists.

Patent (pa-tnt) - A government document that gives an inventor the right to be the only maker of a product for a certain number of years.

Plasma (plaz-muh) - The largest part of blood.

Preserve (pruh-zurv) - To keep safe from injury, loss, or ruin.

Segregation (seh·gruh·gay·shn) - Setting one group of people apart from another group. Most of the time one group was treated unfairly.

Sharecropping (shehr-kraa-puhng) - Farmers had to give the landowner a portion of their crop.

Survey (sur-vey) - To determine the shape and area of land by measuring with special tools.

Telegraph (teh-luh-graf) - A device that lets people send messages using code and electronics.

Transfusion (tranz·fyoo·zhn) - How blood is transferred

Underground Railroad - A method that helped enslaved people escape from the South to the North during the mid-1800s.

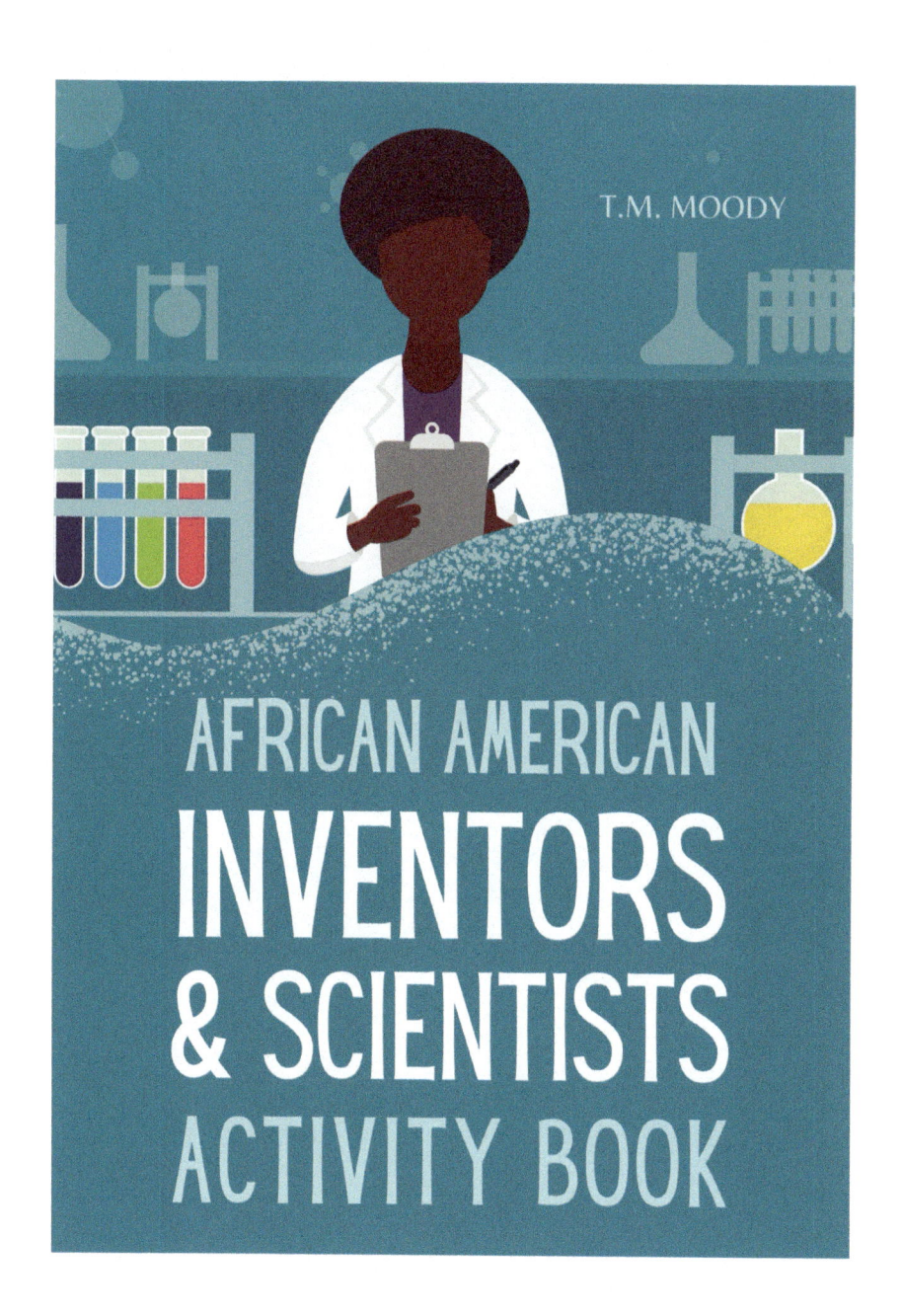

AFRICAN AMERICAN INVENTORS & SCIENTISTS ACTIVITY BOOK

T.M. MOODY

ACTIVITY BOOK

Do you like coloring or puzzles?

Be sure to check out *African American Inventors & Scientists Activity Book*. The activity book includes over 45 activities like coloring, word search, crossword puzzles, mazes, and more.

Download free puzzles at <u>TheKultureKidz.com</u> or try a few sample puzzles on the next few pages.

BENJAMIN BANNEKER WORD SEARCH

Can you find all the hidden words?

L	R	E	H	T	A	E	W	A	W	E	V	D	O
L	R	A	M	N	S	L	S	S	R	E	N	L	I
T	N	X	N	A	K	T	A	A	A	T	E	R
N	N	H	A	C	R	P	A	U	L	T	O	E	L
N	T	M	O	O	A	L	N	V	E	Y	K	Y	A
O	S	L	N	G	P	A	C	S	U	R	E	L	A
N	C	O	L	A	K	N	R	G	N	E	M	S	S
S	M	P	M	R	N	E	A	A	H	A	M	U	R
Y	U	A	O	Y	V	T	O	L	N	L	N	T	Y
Y	Y	H	O	I	L	S	C	A	M	N	N	E	N
R	S	Y	N	S	R	N	C	X	S	A	V	L	V
R	U	U	H	S	A	A	A	Y	A	R	R	S	R
L	S	T	A	R	S	T	L	E	U	N	S	L	R
O	N	K	T	N	U	M	A	S	L	S	A	C	A

WORD LIST

Clock Astronomy Almanac Universe
Planets Stars Galaxy Moon
Sun Weather Survey Land

©TheKultureKidz.com

GEORGE WASHINGTON CARVER MAZE

Carver learned growing peanuts helped nourish the soil for the next cotton crop. Solve the maze below.

ABOUT THE AUTHOR

T.M. Moody has a deep love for history and started the Kulture Kidz website in 1999. She has worked for over twenty years as an education content creator and digital curator in public media. Her specialty is creating interactive, standards-based content for the K-12 community.

Moody also has been an author for over ten years. She writes mysteries under her real name, Tyora Moody.

KULTURE KIDZ BOOKS

Kulture Kidz Books creates content and books for ages 6-12. Our mission is to learn about people who made a difference.

For this book's bibliography, visit https://thekulturekidz.com/bibliographies/

Made in the USA
Monee, IL
17 December 2022